Conferencing and Reporting
Second Edition

By Kathleen Gregory, Caren Cameron, Anne Davies

A Joint Publication

Solution Tree

Connections
Publishing

Published in the US by Solution Tree Press
555 North Morton Street
Bloomington, IN 47404
800.733.6786 (toll free) / 812.336.7700
FAX: 812.336.7790

email: info@solution-tree.com
solution-tree.com

Printed in the United States of America

15 14 13 12 11   1 2 3 4 5

FSC
Mixed Sources
Product group from well-managed
forests and other controlled sources
Cert no. SW-COC-002283
www.fsc.org
© 1996 Forest Stewardship Council

Library of Congress Cataloging-in-Publication Data

Gregory, Kathleen.
  Conferencing and reporting / by Kathleen Gregory, Caren Cameron, Anne Davies. – 2nd ed.
      p. cm.
  Includes bibliographical references.
  ISBN 978-1-935543-79-4 (perfect bound) – ISBN 978-1-935543-80-0 (library edition) 1. Student-led parent conferences. 2. Parent-teacher conferences. 3. Students–Self-rating of. 4. Teacher-student relationships. I. Cameron, Caren. II. Davies, Anne, 1955- III. Title.
  LC225.5.G74 2011
  371.102'3–dc22
                                        2011008259

Solution Tree
Jeffrey C. Jones, CEO & President

Solution Tree Press
President: Douglas M. Rife
Publisher: Robert D. Clouse
Vice President of Production: Gretchen Knapp
Managing Production Editor: Caroline Wise
Senior Production Editor: Risë Koben

Connections Publishing
Stewart Duncan, CEO & President
Project Manager: Judith Hall-Patch
Design: Karen Armstrong, Mackenzie Duncan, Kelly Giordano, Cori Jones

Acknowledgments

Annalee Greenberg, thank you for being our editor over all these years, in spite of delays. We would also like to thank Karen Armstrong and Pat Stanton for their graphic design expertise. A special thanks to our friend and colleague, Colleen Politano, with whom our conversations about involving learners in assessment practices all began.

—Kathleen Gregory, Caren Cameron, and Anne Davies

Contents

3. Questions and Responses   53

What do you think of districts that mandate involvement of students in conferencing and reporting? /**53** Aren't students reluctant to have parents come to school or to talk about what they are doing in school? /**53** How can I do student-parent-teacher conferences when I have over 100 students? /**54** How do you possibly find time to do all the ideas described in this book? /**56** How do you help parents respond to their child's work in a positive, constructive manner? /**57** Is it worth it to involve students in assessment? /**57** How can we get busy parents more involved? /**58**

Foreword

Over the past 20 years, we have experienced a revolution in our understanding about how to communicate about student learning in ways that support that learning. Among the most powerful options, we now understand, are students telling the story of their own growth while they're learning, and students reporting to others about their achievement status with evidence to back up their claims. In this brief but strategy-packed book, Anne, Kathleen, and Caren show teachers exactly how to take full advantage of these options.

Conferencing and Reporting provides practical strategies for engaging students as partners in (1) initiating and conducting conversations about their learning, and (2) conferencing with others about their learning success, whereby they become partners in telling their own story. Not only have Anne, Kathleen, and Caren's offerings (originally published in 2001) stood the test of a decade of application, but, in the interim, a strong and rapidly growing body of research has risen to corroborate their contention that these strategies have a profoundly positive impact on student learning. (For details, see Hattie & Timperley, 2007.)

Before launching into the study of these offerings, it is very important that the reader understand the circumstances that make it possible for student-involved assessment, record keeping, and communication to make their unique and powerful contribution to learning. Those essential conditions turn the classroom into an environment in which students are helped to gain a sense of control over their own academic well-being—that is, a sense of academic self-efficacy, if you will. Professor Albert Bandura has studied self-efficacy as a generalized psychological characteristic that can be defined as a continuum from strong to weak. The two paragraphs that follow describe both ends of that span in those generalized terms. But educators can think of this in academic terms. When applied consistently day-to-day in the classroom, the strategies described herein can move students boldly toward the strong end of the academic self-efficacy continuum, by building students' sense of control over their own academic well-being.

A strong sense of efficacy enhances human accomplishment and personal well-being in many ways. People with high assurance in their capabilities approach difficult tasks as challenges to be mastered rather than as threats to be avoided. They set themselves challenging goals and maintain strong commitment to them, becoming deeply engrossed in learning, and heightening and sustaining their efforts in the face of failure.

They quickly recover their sense of efficacy after failures or setbacks, attributing failure to insufficient effort or deficient knowledge and skills which are acquirable. . . .

In contrast, people who doubt their capabilities shy away from difficult tasks, which they view as personal threats. They have low aspirations and weak commitment to the goals they choose to pursue. When faced with difficult tasks, they dwell on their personal deficiencies and anticipate obstacles and adverse outcomes, rather than concentrating on how to perform successfully. They not only slacken their efforts and give up quickly, but are slow to recover their sense of efficacy following failure or setbacks. Viewing their insufficient performance as deficient aptitude, they quickly lose faith in their own capabilities. (Bandura, 1994, p. 71)

To understand how Anne, Kathleen, and Caren's strategies support the development in students of a strong sense of internal control of learning, consider their first entry in initiating conversations about learning: Work Samples. In this case, students compile samples of their work that are illustrative of changes in their own capabilities. This process requires that they understand the learning target and performance criteria well enough to see and understand those changes. They select two pieces of their work that reveal improvements and prepare to share those, along with their evaluations of each piece, as evidence of their learning, with someone whose opinion of them they care about—parents, peers, teachers, and others. While they may not have progressed all the way to the learning destination, they can watch themselves moving ever closer, and thus maintain the sense of optimism needed to keep going.

A GPS (global positioning system) is an apt metaphor for understanding this process. When one uses a GPS in an automobile, boat, or plane, one lays a solid foundation for success in traveling to a desired destination. One enters that destination and the current location. The computer calculates waypoints along the journey and tracks progress from waypoint to waypoint, keeping the traveler informed of current location. The conferencing and reporting strategies offered herein represent a GPS for student learning success. Teachers determine and share with their students the learning destination. Together, they use the classroom assessment process to determine where the student is now. Then, working as a team, they mark the waypoints as the student travels, ultimately arriving at the destination—learning success. These strategies for conversing about learning represent various kinds of travel logs to achievement.

The reader should think of the section on student-involved conferences as a celebration of arrival at the destination and a determination of where we go next in the learning. In truth, I have watched parents moved to tears with pride and surprise at what they see their child demonstrating in a student-led conference. They see and hear their child revealing capabilities they had no idea she or he possessed. The authors provide clear and specific instructions for what to do in preparation for, during, and after conferences to leave learners feeling pride at what has been accomplished, as well as a connection between that and their plans for what comes next in their learning.

For decades, we have operated on the assumption that assessment is something teachers *do to* students. We have believed that, if we just get the right evidence into teachers' hands, they will make all of the right instructional decisions and schools will become increasingly effective. These beliefs aren't wrong, but they are insufficient, ignoring the reality that students are data-based instructional decision-makers, too. Learners interpret their own evidence and decide, for example, whether the target is within reach for them and whether to take the risk of trying. As educators, our collective oversight is not realizing that students get to make their decisions first. Ultimately, it doesn't matter what teachers decide. If the student gives up, the learning stops. This book is about helping students make productive decisions about continuing to pursue academic success. When they do, achievement skyrockets. I encourage readers to take full advantage of the tools offered herein.

Rick Stiggins
Assessment Training Institute
Portland, OR

References

Bandura, A. (1994). Self-efficacy. In V. S. Rama-chaudran (Ed.), *Encyclopedia of Human Behavior* (Vol. 4, pp. 71–81). New York: Academic Press.

Hattie, J. & H. Timperley. (2007). The power of feedback. *Review of Educational Research*, *77*(1), 81–112.

Introduction

Conferencing and reporting are changing.

The process of conferencing and reporting is changing from a teacher-directed, end-of-term event to a collaborative, ongoing process designed to support learning. Many educators and parents now recognize conferencing and reporting are taking place when:

- students show and talk about work samples with someone at home

- parents look at their daughter's website and respond to her by pointing out their favorite parts and asking questions

- an uncle comes to view a nephew's portfolio during a portfolio afternoon and writes a note telling three things he noticed about the work

- students invite their former kindergarten teacher to a poetry performance where they demonstrate their skill

- student, parents, and teacher meet to look at student work and to set new goals

Parents, students, and teachers are identifying conferencing and reporting practices that effectively communicate and support student learning.

These practices have the following characteristics:

- Students take a lead role.
- Work samples or demonstrations are used to show proof of learning.
- Students invite an audience to participate in the process.
- Audiences take active roles and give specific feedback to learners.

Students take a lead role.

Students who take a lead role in conferencing and reporting prepare by collecting work samples, selecting favorite pieces to talk about, and reflecting on their learning. They show, talk about, and demonstrate their learning to an invited audience. They ask their audience for information about their learning that will help them improve. They participate as active partners in the conferencing and reporting process.

Audiences are essential to the process.

Having an audience students know and care about gives them a purpose for collecting work samples, talking about their learning, and showing their skills. When audiences take an active role, they give specific feedback to students to support learning. Audiences for conferencing and reporting often go beyond parents and guardians to include relatives, family friends, coaches, previous teachers, community members, future employers, or experts in a field. Anyone who is interested in the student's learning and is important to the student can be an audience.

Supporting student learning

Research shows that when students are involved in the assessment process—learning to articulate what they have learned and what they still need to work on—achievement improves (Black & Wiliam, 1998; Stiggins, 2001). When they are offered choices, students are motivated (Jensen, 1998; Kohn, 1999). In addition, learners are supported when they have an audience who shows a genuine interest in their learning (Henderson & Berla, 1995; Werner & Smith, 1992) and offers descriptive (nonjudgmental) feedback (Sutton, 1997; Wiggins, 1993). Finally, when students communicate their learning using a variety of work samples, they go beyond what grades, numbers, and scores alone can show; they are able to examine the depth, the detail, and the range of their own learning. From this information, they identify their strengths and what they need to work on next.

In this book, we describe ways of conferencing and reporting that support student learning. In chapter 1, we describe ten ways of conferencing and reporting where students initiate conversations about their own learning at any time during the term. In chapter 2, we describe three ways of conferencing and reporting that bring together students, parents, and teachers to review the learning that has taken place over a term. In chapter 3, we respond to common questions and concerns from students, teachers, administrators, and parents.

We recognize the variety of policies related to conferencing and reporting that teachers are required to follow. Therefore, we invite you to select any ideas that interest you and fit your context; please adapt rather than adopt these to make them work for you and your students.

1. Initiating Conversations About Learning

In this chapter, we describe ten ideas that show how students can initiate informal conversations about their own learning. These conversations:

- are planned at school by students with teacher support

- take place between a student and an audience outside of school

- take place anytime during the year

- communicate learning in concrete ways that go beyond numbers and grades

- invite an audience to respond to the learning

We offer specific steps that prepare students to take lead roles in the conferencing and reporting process. We provide samples of student reflection and audience response, as well as adaptations that have worked for us and for our colleagues.

Please notice my improvement in _Silkscreening_
In sample #1
(Oct. 13) I didn't know how to silkscreen. It was hard to cut it to get it to look right.
In sample #2
(Oct. 28) The colors are clear and it didn't get all streaky.
Nick

Response
I notice your improvement...
in the color and I really liked your Hallowe'en design.
Other comments:
Keep up the good work! I know that you love doing this.
Love Mom (Dorothy C.)

Figure 1:
Work samples

Work Samples

Students choose work samples to take home that show growth in their learning. They show and talk with an audience about the samples and ask for a response to their work.

1. Tell students they will need to keep samples of their work over the term, for example, when doing science labs, tests, writing, mapping, or problem solving.

2. Have students select two work samples of similar tasks that show some improvement.

3. Ask students to think of someone who might be interested in seeing and responding to their work. Give them self-assessment forms that highlight their improvement (see figure 1).

4. Ask students to take home these samples to an audience who completes the response section.

ADAPTATIONS

When we know that parents are interested in seeing more of a specific skill, such as spelling or math computation, we structure the work samples so that they can see improvements.

Students have the option of bringing these work samples and responses back to the school to include in their portfolios or of keeping them at home.

Portfolio Afternoon

Students collect work samples over the term and organize them into a portfolio. They write personal comments about each piece, explaining why they've selected it and what they want others to notice. Teachers schedule a time for a portfolio afternoon. Students invite someone who is important to them to come and view their portfolios. Invited guests provide feedback to the learners.

1. At the beginning of the term, talk with students about keeping samples of their work so they can see and show others evidence of their learning.

2. During the term, have students keep a variety of work so they have a selection to choose from when they create their portfolios.

3. Have each student select pieces to put in his or her portfolio. It helps to give students a table of contents. They then select pieces that correspond to the items listed (see figure 2).

Figure 2: Portfolio table of contents
Reproducible in appendix, page 62

Subject _Social Studies 10_	
Name _John Michael_	
Table of Contents for _My portfolio_	
Select samples that show	**Your sample**
☑ a strength	test on WW II (88%)
☑ improvement	using different types of sources (bibliography)
☑ successful collaboration	group map project
☑ originality	poster - front page headline
☑ other _debate_	Andrea's comment sheet

Two reasons I chose this piece...

- I now can write a bibliography correctly

- I used Encarta, a book, and the video on W.W II

Date____Jan. 12^th____   Signed____John____

Please notice:

☐ Favorite
☐ Improvement
☐ Trash it!
☑ Challenge
☐ _____

I selected this piece
because it was really
hard and I've never
done this before.

Date____Oct. 17^th____   Signed____Donnie____

Figure 3:
Student comments

4. Have students record a comment on each piece they have selected by completing a form that tells what they want others to notice about their work (see figure 3).

5. Work together as a class to brainstorm guests they might like to invite as an audience to this portfolio afternoon (see figure 4).

6. Have students write an invitation to one or more individuals they choose from this list (see figure 5).

7. Give time in class for students to rehearse by showing and talking about their portfolios with a peer.

8. Reserve a space, such as the library, for an afternoon.

Possible Guests

parents/step parents

former principals and teachers

relatives (aunts, uncles, grandparents)

school staff (janitor, secretary, other teachers, librarian, counsellor)

sports coaches

family friends

**Figure 4:
Brainstorm list
of people**

DATE

Dear _____

On _____ my class will be sharing our
      DATE
portfolios with parents and other special guests.

On this day, we are asking you to

- come to the _____ at _____
            PLACE   TIME

- view my portfolio with me

- comment on the samples of work I've selected to show you

When you come, I'd like you to notice

-

-

-

Please let me know if you can come so I can let

_____ know.
    TEACHER

           Yours truly,

        _____
           SIGNATURE

**Figure 5:
Invitation form
for portfolio
afternoon**

9.   Arrange with students for refreshments.

10. At the portfolio afternoon, ask students to introduce their guests to you as they arrive.

11. Have students show and talk about their portfolios with their invited guests. Ask guests to complete a response card before leaving (see figure 6).

Figure 6:
Response card
Reproducible in appendix,
page 63

Portfolio Afternoon **Audience Response**

Two compliments I have for _____*Kate*_____ :

- *You really put a lot of effort into your work*
- *I really liked the memoir you wrote about your grandfather in the war*

Something I would like to see next time:

- *More of the same - keep up the good work!*

Date____*Feb. 21*____   Signed____*Mrs. Wiltenburg*____

12. Following the portfolio afternoon, ask students to review the event by asking questions such as "What worked?" "What didn't?" and "What could we do another time?"

ADAPTATIONS

When parents or other audiences are unable to attend, we suggest students make an appointment with someone to view their portfolio outside of school time (see Home Performances, p. 33).

Sometimes we support students who need assistance during the portfolio afternoon by sitting in on parts of their conversations.

Some students choose to invite other parents and guests to view their portfolios and to complete a comment card.

Goal Envelopes

Students set a personal goal they want to achieve. They collect evidence to put in an envelope to show an audience how they are meeting or have met their goal. Students choose a time, place, and audience to present what they have accomplished.

1. Work with students to set personal goals. Pose questions such as "What do you want to be able to do in this class by the end of the term?" "What skill do you want to improve?" and "What's the one thing you'd like to try doing in this course that you've never done before?" (For more information on setting goals, see chapter 2 of *Self-Assessment and Goal Setting,* the second book in this series.)

2. Show students a sample of a completed goal envelope. Explain that having someone to show their evidence to keeps them focused on their goal; keeping evidence reminds them that they are moving forward (see figure 7).

3. Give each student a nine-by-twelve-inch envelope to which you have attached a form, such as the one in figure 7. Every few weeks give students time in class to collect evidence related to their goal.

4. Provide time for students to show and talk about their evidence with partners.

5. Look at what students have included in their envelopes. Then have them show someone outside of school how they have met or are working toward their goal.

6. Have students ask their audience to respond on the envelope.

Goal Envelope for _____Jill_____   **Response from** ___Mrs. C.___

Term ___1___ Subject(s) ___Math___

My goal for this term is _____
to get my math homework done for
the rest of the term

My evidence shows I
☐ am working toward my goal
☑ have met my goal

1. _my agenda book is signed_
2. _see my notebook (homework is completed)_
3. _the comment on my report card_

Congratulations on:
-all the homework you
did this month

-bringing your agenda
book home for me to
sign

Next time:

keep up the great
work – it pays off!

Term _____ Subject(s) _____

My goal for this term is _____
_____
_____

My evidence shows I
☐ am working toward my goal
☐ have met my goal

1. _____
2. _____
3. _____

Response from _____

Congratulations on:
-

-

Next time:

Figure 7: Goal envelope
Reproducible in appendix, page 64

ADAPTATIONS

Some colleagues ask their students to show goal envelopes during parent-teacher conferences.

Subject Stations

Students complete specific projects or tasks in class. During the year, they invite guests to come to school to see these projects. The guests look at all the projects, ask questions, and give specific comments.

1. As a class, develop a guest list of people whom students want to invite to see their individual or group projects.

2. Organize a time and place for students to show their projects.

3. Have each student choose one or two people from the list to invite. Provide students with invitation forms to complete. Mail these or have students deliver them (see figure 8).

4. On the day of the event, ask students to set up their projects in designated areas or stations, numbered to make it easier for guests to move from one to another.

Figure 8: Subject station invitation

Dear Mr. Boardman ,

I would like you to come and see the project on

ecosystems that I have been working

on in class.

Date Feb. 22

Time 2:00—3:00 P.M.

Place Treebank School Library

When you come, I'd especially like you to notice that

- I worked with Mike and Jan
- We finished everything
- We made a model

Please let me know if you can come.

Yours truly,

Kelsey

5. Have students introduce their guests to you as they arrive. Give guests a response sheet to complete as they visit each station.

6. Have students invite their guests to begin at their own stations; then have guests circulate to other stations.

7. Have guests complete responses for each station they have time to visit (see figure 9).

8. Collect response sheets as guests leave.

9. The next day, give students the responses from their guests for their own stations. Ask them for their own reaction to the event by asking questions such as "What was the best part?" "What would we change next time?" and "What surprised you?"

Figure 9:
Subject station
response sheet

Subject Stations Response Sheet

Station #4
Comment: I never knew there were so many animals in the Arctic. You are a fine artist!
Question: How long did this take you?
Signed Kevin's Aunt Anna

Station #6
Comment: I never thought of the human body as an ecosystem before.
Question: Where did you get the idea from?
Signed Kevin's Aunt Anna

Station #
Comment:
Question:
Signed

Station #
Comment:
Question:
Signed

ADAPTATIONS

Some colleagues have had great success with stations featuring research projects, woodwork design projects, web pages, and video productions.

Picture This

Students select or are given photos that have been taken of them in class. They then write about the learning that is captured in the picture.

1. Take photos of students in class as they work on specific projects or tasks, such as working through a science process, working on group projects, presenting an oral report, or showing a finished display or art project.

2. Give students a photo of themselves. Have them complete a form that tells an audience about the learning shown in the photo (see figure 10).

Picture This

There is more to this picture than you can see. This is a photo of _me in character in my first stage role._

I/We want you to notice that:

- putting on the makeup took about three hours
- that is all my own hair!
- I learned how much of yourself you have to put into your character to make it really believable.

Date _Jan. 20_   Signed _Anthony_

**Figure 10:
Picture This**
Reproducible in appendix, page 65

3. Ask students to show the photo and the completed write-up to someone at home.

4. Have students talk about the photo and ask their audience questions such as "What did you notice?" and "What do you want to know more about?"

ADAPTATIONS

We give students the option of bringing the photos back to school to put in their portfolios or of keeping them at home.

Some colleagues use audio or video recordings instead of photographs.

Criteria for problem-solving	Specifics
understand the problem and choose a strategy to solve it	- use diagrams to figure it out, or you can use objects - you can tell when a part is missing (need more information) - talk it through with someone (read it aloud) - try a bunch of ways until it works - think of other problems you've worked on that are similar and do that - break the problem down into steps
compute accurately	- do steps in the right order - get it right - check it - the answer has to make sense
explain to someone how you reached your solution	- when you are finished, you can tell someone how you arrived at your answer - be able to explain how you did it
connect to an example outside the classroom	- think of a job where you'd use this (we use the same idea when we buy carpet for our house)

Figure 11a: T-chart of criteria

Criteria With Evidence

Students take home a work sample, with a list of criteria developed in class. They explain the criteria to an audience. They point out where in their assignment they have met the criteria as well as what they still need to work on. They then ask their audience for a response.

1. Teacher and students develop criteria for an activity. Teacher poses the question, "What's important in . . . ?" Students and teacher brainstorm a list of the important features of the particular assignment, sort and categorize these ideas, and make a T-chart (see figure 11a, opposite). (For further information on setting criteria, see *Setting and Using Criteria,* the first book in this series.)

2. Have students take home an assignment that they have selected and the teacher has assessed in relation to the criteria (see figures 11a and 11b).

Criteria for problem solving	Met	Not Yet Met
understand the problem and choose a strategy to solve it	✓	
compute accurately		✓
explain to someone how you reached your solution	✓	
connect to an example outside the classroom		✓

Figure 11b: Criteria

3. Ask students to explain the criteria to an audience at home, showing where they have met or not yet met criteria.

4. Ask audience to complete a checklist response to indicate how well they understood the criteria (see figure 12).

Response from _____	It's Clear	It's Not Clear
1. After reading the criteria, I understand what was required in the assignment		
2. The criteria helped me see what you've done well		
3. I can see what you need to work on next		

Comments: _____

_____

_____

_____

_____

Figure 12: Checklist response
Reproducible in appendix, page 66

Mind Maps

Students create mind maps in class. They choose an audience and show and talk to them about their mind maps. The audience listens, asks questions, and responds.

1. In front of the class, make a mind map, thinking aloud during the process. This will model the process of creating a mind map.

2. Ask students questions such as "What did you learn from listening to my thinking and looking at my mind map?" "What part of my thinking is clear to you?" "What part is not clear?" and "What else would you have added to the mind map that I haven't included?"

3. Give students time in class to create their own mind maps (see figure 13) to illustrate their understanding of an idea (for example, photosynthesis, early man, congressional system, medieval warfare, story map). Provide opportunities for students to share their mind maps with a peer.

4. Have each student select a favorite mind map that he or she has created to show and talk about with an audience outside of the class.

5. After showing the mind map, students pose questions such as "What did you learn from listening to my thinking and looking at my mind map?" "What part of my thinking was clear to you?" "What part was not clear?" and "What would you add to my mind map that I haven't included?"

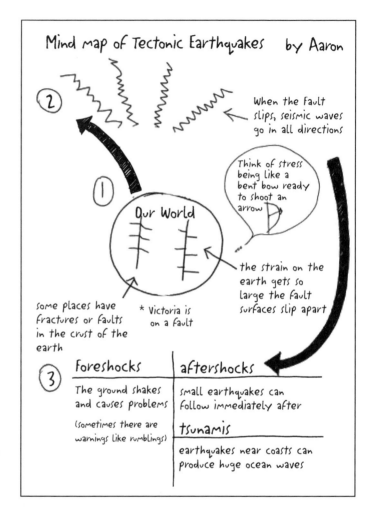

Figure 13: Mind map

ADAPTATIONS

One colleague asks students to complete a mind map at the beginning of a unit of study using one color of ink and then has them repeat the process at the end of the study using a different color of ink. When students show and talk with an audience about their before-and-after mind maps, they point out what they have learned.

Home Performances

Students perform a skill at home for family members. The audience listens and comments on the performance.

1. Ask students to arrange to perform a specific task or skill they have learned in class (for example, a cooking or art technique, poetry presentation, movement exercise, computer or sports skill) for someone at home.

2. Give students a form to complete that highlights three things the performer would like the audience to observe (see figure 14).

3. At the time of the performance, have students give their audience the form, explaining what they would like them to observe. Students perform their task or skill.

4. After the performance, students ask their audience for a response.

Figure 14: Home performance

Home Performance by _____Reg_____

I am going to _play four Strong Winds on the guitar_

Please notice:

- that this piece is easy to play

- I know 4 chords — C G7 Dm7 F

- I can change chords quickly.

Date_ April 11 _

Audience Response by_____ Alanna _____

After listening to and watching your performance I'd like to compliment you on: _excellent playing of the piece and playing it all the way through._

I'd also like to add: _You are getting better._

_____

School Performances

When students introduce school performances, they tell the audience what skills they will be observing. Members of the audience are asked to give specific feedback to the performers.

1. Have students hand out school performance response sheets as the audience enters. One or more students introduces the school performance (such as a band concert, drama production, debate tournament, Readers Theater, gymnastics demonstration) by outlining the specific skills involved. Have students tell the audience what to notice about the performance (see figure 15).

2. After the performance, have students ask the audience to complete and hand in their responses before leaving and thank them for attending. (see figure 15).

School Performance: Poetry Presentation

Please notice:

Preparation
Students had memorized their poems.

Attitude
Students were enthusiastic and enjoyed themselves.

Organization
Students knew when it was their turn and they worked to keep the presentation moving smoothly.

A note to the performers from Mr. Powell (granddad)

Your presentation was great! I loved the poems people selected. It's great to see you enjoying yourselves and practicing speaking in front of others.

Figure 15: Audience response to school performance

Personal Newsletter

Students use a newsletter format to write about their learning. They select an audience to give their newsletters to and ask for specific feedback.

1. Give students a sample of a personal newsletter (this may be written by a former student or be a sample you create). Have a discussion about the purposes for communicating learning with others and about possible contents of the newsletter.

2. Pose the question, "Who do you know (who is older than you) who you think would be interested in receiving your personal newsletter?" As a group, develop a class list of people.

3. From this list, have each student choose the audience for his or her newsletter.

4. Offer students planning frames to help get them started (see figure 16).

5. Give students time in class to complete newsletters during the term. You may want to have them design a response form for the audience to complete.

6. Invite students to include some excerpts from their newsletters in their portfolios.

> Headline: Drew Does Drama
> Byline: Drew C.
> Dateline: March 15, Saanich
>
> So far in __Drama 10__ we have worked on the following:
> - improv-
> - script reading
> - blocking
>
> I'm good at improv, especially when Matt and I did the Archie Andrews skit.
>
> I'm getting better at relaxing
>
> I need to improve my focus
>
> Something I hope to do more of is performing in the school theater
>
> One word that describes my effort in class is "Excellent!!"
>
> One thing I'd like to add is I really enjoyed the standing ovation we got.

Figure 16: Personal newsletter
Reproducible in appendix, page 67

ADAPTATIONS

Some students communicate their learning by having structured e-mail conversations with their parents or family members.

2. Involving Students in Conferences

In this chapter, we describe three types of conferences in which students review the learning that has taken place over a term. The first conference we describe extends the idea of a parent-teacher conference by having students, parents, and teachers all taking on active roles in the process. The second conference we describe involves students with special needs who have individual education plans (IEPs). The third type of conference, between a teacher and student, requires the student to demonstrate learning in relation to course goals or standards. Each type of conference:

- is scheduled by the teacher, held at the school, and follows a formal agenda

- has students prepare for and take on a lead role

- reviews the learning at the end of the term by using samples of student work

- has each participant take an active role in the process

- may include a written summary report

For each way of conferencing and reporting, we describe logistical issues, outline specific roles for each participant, and provide samples of forms, brochures, and agendas. For each idea, we offer adaptations that have worked for our colleagues and for us.

Student-Parent-Teacher Conference

Teachers schedule a fifteen- to twenty-minute time frame when students, parents or guardians, and teachers meet together to review the learning that has taken place during the term. Each participant comes prepared to take an active part. A summary of this conference can provide information for report-card comments or become a written report.

Student-Parent-Teach
Conferences

HILLCREST
School

Figure 17: Brochure for student-parent-teacher conference

Reproducibles in appendix, pages 68 and 69

Hillcrest School

Dear Parents/Guardians,

You are invited to attend a conference on _____
DATE

At this time, the student, parent(s) and teacher(s) will meet together to talk about the learning that has taken place during the term. The conference will take 15 minutes. Your son/daughter knows a great deal about his/her own learning and has collected work samples to show you.

By working together, we can support your son or daughter's learning. I look forward to seeing you at the conference.

Yours truly,

_____
TEACHER SIGNATURE

Format

The number one purpose of the conference is to support the learning of your son or daughter by:

1. Talking about strengths and areas of progress
2. Looking at and discussing work samples
3. Talking about areas needing improvement
4. Setting one or two goals for next term
5. Discussing ways to help meet goals

* A written summary of the conversation will be sent home

Please return this portion

_____
Student's name

_____
Parent's name

Preferred days

☐ _____

☐ _____

Preferred time

☐ _____

☐ _____

PROCEDURE

Before the conference

Early in the term

1. Tell students they will be participating in a student-parent-teacher conference. Emphasize why it is important for them to participate. Give students an idea of how such a conference works by reviewing the brochure that will be sent to parents (see figure 17).

During the term

1. Give students time to collect a range of work samples to show at the conference.

2. Have them record a comment about why they selected each piece of work.

Two weeks or so before the conference

1. Send a brochure home to parents. Ask them to fill in and return the brochure's tear-off portion to the school.

2. Give students a sheet to complete that summarizes their learning (see figure 18).

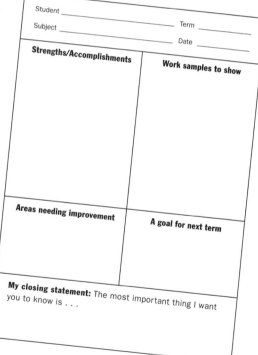

Figure 18: Student summary sheet

Reproducible in appendix, page 70

Student _____

Subject _____ Term _____

Date _____

Strengths/Accomplishments

Work samples to show

Areas needing improvement

A goal for next term

My closing statement: The most important thing I want you to know is . . .

3. Have students rehearse with a partner what they are going to show and discuss.

4. Send a summary sheet to parents that includes their conference time and information to think about before they attend the student-parent-teacher conference (see figure 19).

Figure 19: Parent summary sheet
Reproducible in appendix, page 71

	Please note your conference is:
	Date _____
Date _____	Time _____

Dear Parents/Guardians,

In preparation for our upcoming conference, please take a few minutes and jot down some ideas about your son or daughter. You might want to include accomplishments that take place outside of school as well as in school.

Yours truly,

_____
(TEACHER SIGNATURE)

Any areas of strength, growth, accomplishments:	One or two areas you'd like to see improvement in:	One specific goal:

P.S. Please bring these notes to the conference for your own use. Please do not send this form back to the school.

5. Complete your own summary sheet for each student (see figure 20).

During the conference

1. Welcome the student and have him or her introduce the parent(s) or guardian(s).

2. Review the format of the conference, noting the time frame and agenda. Let participants know that you will be keeping notes.

3. Invite the student to talk about two or three strengths and show work samples as evidence. Then ask parents to talk about two or three strengths (things their son or daughter does well in or out of school). Conclude by sharing two or three strengths you have observed in the student or provide additional evidence to support the strengths that have already been mentioned.

4. Ask the student to talk about one or two things she or he needs to improve. Then ask the parents to talk about one or two areas they want their son or daughter to improve in. If an important concern has been left out, remind others of previous conversations relating to this concern. Discuss it further.

Figure 20: Teacher summary sheet
Reproducible in appendix, page 72

Teacher Summary Sheet	
Student _____ Term _____	
Subject(s) _____ Date _____	
Areas of strength	**Areas needing improvement**
	Additional notes:
Possible goal(s)	

Summary report for _Liam Rogers_

The following is a summary of our student-parent-teacher conference held on _November 18_

Areas of strength:

- _works well with others and on his own; shows a positive attitude_
- _reading responses and quizzes indicate he understands plot and character development_
- _uses historical terms correctly (score 21/28), poses questions and researches using a variety of sources (project score 45/50) and understands concepts taught (refer to sample of mind map)_
- _understands math concepts taught to date including exponents, geometry, and percentage problems. A typical score on unit reviews is 80%_
- _ecology project shows his interest and skill level in science (score 29/35) this term_

Areas needing improvement:

As we discussed, Liam's notebooks lack organization. Items often go missing and work does not always get handed in on time. For example, in Science, he could have improved his overall grade by keeping his lab notebook up to date and complete.

Goal(s): _To be more organized and hand work in on time_

Plan: _use a binder with dividers for each subject_
use my school planner to record homework

Support: _Parents will check and sign the planner_
Teacher will check to see that Liam has recorded all due dates.

Liam R.   _C. St___   _Marlene Rogers_
STUDENT SIGNATURE   TEACHER SIGNATURE   PARENT SIGNATURE

Figure 21: Summary report

5. Have the student talk about a goal he or she wants to work on and how he or she plans to achieve it. Parent or teacher may suggest an additional goal, remembering that it is important to narrow the focus to one or two specific goals. Decide ways the student can be supported in meeting his or her goals at home and at school. Then ask the student to read a closing statement.

6. Thank the student and the parent(s) for being part of the conference. Let them know how and when the summary report will be communicated.

Figure 22: Parents' response form

Reproducible in appendix, page 73

After the conference

1. Send out the summary report along with a response form for parents to complete (see figures 21 and 22).

2. Review the conference with students (orally or in writing).

3. Use the information from the responses to rethink and refine the process used.

ADAPTATIONS

When the idea of taking part in a conference is new to our students, we prepare them by inviting former students to talk about their experiences with conferences. We also role-play a conference where the teacher takes on the student role.

Parents/Guardians

We need your comments to improve our student-parent-teacher conferences. Thank you for taking the time to complete this form and return it to the school.

Two things you liked about the conference:

_____

_____

One suggestion:

_____

_____

One question:

_____

If students do not have time to show all their evidence during the conference, they are encouraged to take it home. We also invite parents to let us know if they require a separate conference.

If students are supported by other staff in the school, then these individuals often sit in and contribute to the conference.

In some schools the summary report becomes the report card. In other schools it is used as a substitute for the standardized computer comments and is attached to the computer-generated report card.

See page 54 of chapter 3, Questions and Responses, for a variety of scenarios that some teachers use to include some of their students in student-parent-teacher conferences.

Individual Education Plan (IEP) Conference

During the year the student, teacher, parents, and other IEP team members meet to review the individual education plan (IEP). A summary of this meeting, the IEP review, may be used as a basis for reporting.

PROCEDURE

Before the conference

1. Contact all participants to arrange a time and place.

2. Ask participants to complete a summary sheet (see figure 23).

3. Interview the student (and his/her assistant if appropriate), and make notes (see figure 24).

4. Help the student and assistant in collecting work samples to show at the review.

5. Complete your own summary sheet.

6. Prepare an agenda that can be posted or handed out at the conference.

IEP Participant(s) Summary Sheet

Growth & development I've seen:

Practices that work well (at home, at school):

One or two areas to focus on next:

Figure 23: Participants summary sheet for IEP review
Reproducible in appendix, page 74

IEP Interview Questions

What did you like doing this term?

What did your teacher or someone else do that helped you learn?

What projects or pieces of work do you want to show at the conference?

What is one thing you'd like to get better at?

Figure 24: IEP interview questions for students

During the conference

1. Welcome and introduce everyone.

2. Explain the format of the IEP review, and refer participants to the agenda and time frame. Let the group know that you will be taking notes.

3. Invite the student to show and talk about what he or she has enjoyed doing and show favorite work samples. You may need to use questions and prompts to support the student as needed.

4. Invite parents, teacher, and IEP team members to talk about what they have noticed in the growth and development of the student in or out of school. Summarize the discussion, keep notes, and ensure that IEP goals are discussed. Include work samples as evidence when needed.

5. Ask the student what he or she would like to get better at or learn how to do. Then ask the parents and other members of the IEP team what areas they want the student to work on. Summarize the discussion, and mention any other areas that you have concerns about. Ensure that the concerns are reflected in the IEP goals.

6. Invite participants to talk about ways of working with the student that have been effective. Summarize the information for the group.

7. Ask the participants for any reminders that need to be noted, such as referrals or placement decisions.

8. Thank everyone for being part of the review. Let them know that a written summary will be sent out (see figure 25).

After the conference

1. Talk with the student about the conference and the written summary. Ask if he or she has any questions or suggestions.

2. Send the written summary of the review to all IEP team members. Ask for any suggestions or advice to improve subsequent conferences.

Figure 25: Summary of IEP review

Summary of IEP Review

Teacher(s) _____

Student _____ Term _____

Date _____

Effective ways of working with the student:

Specific growth and development:

Recommendations/reminders:

Areas to focus on next:

Student-Teacher Conference

Teachers meet individually with students to review the learning that has taken place. Students lead the conference and present evidence of their learning in relation to goals or standards in a subject or course.

PROCEDURE

Before the conference

Early in the course

1. Explain to students that an individual conference is a course requirement. During the conference, they will show evidence of their learning in relation to each course goal. Tell them that they, not the teacher, will lead the conference.

2. Discuss the sorts of things that show evidence for each goal (see figure 26).

Figure 26:
Course goals

Goals for English Students will:	Possible Evidence
1. read a wide range of materials in different genres	· *list of books read* · *top 10 favorites* · *complete a genre web* · *observations of home reading from others*
2. write responses that show an understanding of what they've read	· *reader response journals* · *selected "best response"* · *self-assessments* · *observations from peers/others*
3. write on a wide range of topics in different forms	· *writing portfolio* · *lists of topics written about* · *writing forms checklist*
4. show an understanding of the rules and conventions of writing (spelling, punctuation, grammar, sentence structure)	· *test scores* · *final publications* · *writing portfolio* · *editing samples*
5. work successfully on their own and in groups	· *peer assessments* · *self-assessments* · *group project results* · *individual assignment grades*

During the course

1. Present a role play of a student-teacher conference, in which the teacher plays the role of the student.

2. Remind students to keep all work they do for the course (in class and outside of class) as evidence of their learning. From time to time, invite volunteers to show and talk about evidence of their learning in relation to a specific goal.

Near the end of the course

1. Arrange a time with each student for a student-teacher conference.

2. Have students prepare a summary sheet of their learning, including a summary statement that they can read or talk about at the conclusion of the conference (see figure 27).

Student _____ *Darren* _____ Term ____ *1* ____	
Subject _____ *English* _____	
Goals for English Students will:	**Evidence of my learning** assignments, self-assessments, observations of others, tests, notebooks:
1. read a wide range of materials in different genres	• *bring in my top 10 books* • *talk about my favorite authors*
2. write responses that show an understanding of what they've read	• *show journal pages of Oct.8, Nov.14*
3. write on a wide range of topics in different forms	• *portfolio* • *show all the forms I've written* *– *my newspaper column*
4. show an understanding of the rules and conventions of writing (spelling, punctuation, grammar, sentence structure)	• *bring my tests and essay*
5. work successfully on their own and in groups	• *bring peer assessments on oral presentation on General Patton*
Summary Statement: *I read harder books than anyone else in this class. I like it best when we choose our own books.*	

Figure 27:
Student summary sheet for student-teacher conference

Student _____Darren_____ Term _____1_____

Subject _____English_____

Goals for English Students will:	Observations (including peer assessments)	Conversations (including self-assessments)	Products (scores, projects, tests)
1. read a wide range of materials in different genres	reads mostly fantasy – challenging material, always has a book		no genre web completed
2. write responses that show an understanding of what they've read	daily response thin		best response score 10/10 missed 5 of 20 responses Met 12 Not yet met 3
3. write on a wide range of topics in different forms		attached self-assessment shows insight, aware of his strengths and knows he doesn't complete everything	some portfolio contents missing (poems & biography) technical writing 40/50 personal writing 15/25
4. show an understanding of the rules and conventions of writing (spelling, punctuation, grammar, sentence structure)	knows rules – rarely chooses to proofread		Tests 25/25 rules, Oct. 2 18/20 grammar, Oct. 17 20/20 sentence combining
5. work successfully on their own and in groups	chooses to work with others whenever possible		group work rubric 3-2-2-1-3 group project 80%

Figure 28: Teacher summary for student-teacher conference

3. Give students time in class to rehearse presenting their evidence and summary statement to a partner.

4. Make your own notes in preparation for the conference (see figure 28).

During the conference

1. Welcome the student. Remind him or her of the purpose of the conference and time allowed. Let the student know that you'll be taking notes.

2. Ask the student to talk about and show evidence of his or her learning.

3. Elicit more information when necessary, prompting with phrases or questions such as "Tell me more about . . . " "I noticed . . . " and "What about . . . ?" Add information from your own assessment data when appropriate.

4. Give students the last word by having them deliver an oral or written summary statement.

5. Thank students for participating. Invite them to complete an anonymous suggestion form.

After the conference

1. Use the notes kept during the conference as part of the overall course evaluation.

2. Look at students' suggestions, reflect on the conference, and refine the process.

ADAPTATIONS

Sometimes, teachers may conduct a student-teacher conference with only one of their classes or with students they need more specific information about.

Some teachers use the conference as a replacement for the final exam and use time during the final exam week schedule to meet with students.

Some students may want to invite someone else to attend the conference as an observer—for example, a peer, a relative, or another teacher.

Some teachers write descriptions for *A*, *B*, and *C* letter grades for their course (see figure 29). They use their conference notes as part of the overall evidence of learning.

Figure 29: Description of an *A*

Description of "A"

Observations, Conversations and Products consistently show evidence of:

- *self-directed readers who select challenging and advanced reading material*
- *insightful readers who produce high-quality entries in their response notebooks*
- *powerful writers who demonstrate skill and flexibility in using a wide variety of formats and forms (depending on purpose and audience)*
- *skilled editors who submit error-free published-level work*
- *collaborative learners who demonstrate their ability to work with others by asking and responding to discussion questions and sharing their personal understanding and connections*

3. Questions and Responses

Q. A neighboring district has mandated involving students in conferencing and reporting. What do you think?

R. That will depend on how the mandated change is being implemented. Everyone involved in the change must have the opportunity and time to shape the idea to make it work for them and their students. This requires a realistic time frame and ongoing support for teachers to make the change. If these conditions are in place, then there is a good chance the district will have success involving students in conferencing and reporting.

Q. Aren't students reluctant to have parents come to school or to talk about what they are doing in school?

R. As students age, they typically show an increasing need for independence from their parents. To encourage them to have conversations about their learning with parents and other adults, we offer them as many age-appropriate choices as possible. We give them time in class to prepare to take a lead role; they choose the samples of work they want to show; they often decide whom they will choose for an audience and what they will say about their learning. We want students to take small steps toward independence as well as develop a sense of responsibility for their own learning.

Q. How can I do student-parent-teacher conferences when I have over 100 students?

R. When we conduct student-parent-teacher conferences, as described in this book, we limit ourselves to approximately thirty students (even though the total number of students some teach is often over 100). The following scenarios offer some possibilities to consider.

Scenario 1: One class only. Some teachers have student-parent-teacher conferences with only one class of students they teach. You may want to choose a group that you think will be receptive to the idea.

Scenario 2: Volunteers. Another way to manage a large number of students is to limit conferences to students who volunteer to participate. When only a few students in a class take part in student-parent-teacher conferences, we still have all of the students collect work samples. We use this evidence of learning at parent-teacher conferences. Working with individuals who choose to attend a conference with their parents is a safe beginning step. When more than thirty students volunteer, we work out a way to include each person in a conference with parents some time during the school year.

Scenario 3: Specific students. You may want to select three or four specific students from each of the classes you teach to take part in student-parent-teacher conferences. It might be individuals who are struggling, students who are excelling, or learners who might need to gain confidence. This approach works when *all* students in the class collect and comment on work samples throughout the term. We do not want to single out a few students and require them to do additional work just because they have been selected to be part of the conference. The students who attend the conference show their samples to parents. When students do not attend the conference, the teacher shows their samples.

Scenario 4: Teaching teams (partners). Some schools make student-parent-teacher conferences possible by having existing teaching teams divide up the total number of students they teach. For example, a group of sixty students may have one teacher for English and social studies and one for math and science. The two teachers will each have thirty students to see at the conference. In our experience, being part of a team involves sharing information about students. In this situation, both teachers have confidence in their knowledge of each student.

Scenario 5: Teaching teams (four or more). A team of four teachers can also divide up a group of 120 students whom they all teach. One drawback can be that teachers may not know all students well enough to be specific about achievement in each subject area to be able to respond to parent questions. When teams of teachers and students stay together for two to three years (as in many teacher advisory systems), teachers know students well enough to make this approach a success. When questions arise about matters best addressed by a specific subject-area teacher, parents are encouraged to speak to the teacher.

Scenario 6: Choose parents. When we first started to include students in student-parent-teacher conferences, we invited only those parents we knew fairly well to attend with their son or daughter. Often we had taught siblings, and a trust had already been established, so we felt comfortable about taking on a new process together.

Parents and students gave us honest and helpful feedback to help us refine a process that was new to us.

There are numerous scenarios being used to involve learners in student-parent-teacher conferences. Each has specific strengths and drawbacks. We invite you to consider how you can best involve learners given your context.

Q. How do you possibly find time to do all of the ideas described in this book?

R. We don't have time to do everything. This book is a collection of ideas we've used over many years. We encourage you to select one or two ideas that catch your interest, are appropriate for your students, and fit within the structure of your school. We want to emphasize that no matter which ideas you choose to try, start with small steps such as:

- sending home work samples
- trying out student-teacher-parent conferences with one or two students with interested parents
- beginning with one class or one subject area

We also recognize there is never enough time to do all we want and need to do in teaching, so we each must decide what we are going to stop doing. We try to let go of the activities that take up time and do little to improve student learning so that we can focus on activities that do support learning.

Q. How do you help parents respond to their child's work in a positive, constructive manner?

R. Many parents do not know how to respond to their children's work in ways that support learning. As a result, when we ask parents for feedback, we offer beginning phrases to complete, such as "Two things I liked are . . . " and "One piece of advice I have is . . . " We also provide information in school newsletters highlighting the importance of parents' role as an audience, of listening and asking questions, and of giving descriptive feedback. However, some parents will continue to respond in ways that don't support their sons' or daughters' learning, so we offer a variety of possible audiences and leave the final decision of *who* the audience will be to our students.

Q. Involving students sounds like a lot of extra work. Is it worth it?

R. Black and Wiliam (1998) conducted a meta-analysis examining classroom assessment that supports student learning. One key conclusion is that when teachers involve students in assessment practices, "the gains in achievement are the largest ever reported for educational interventions" (p. 67). Our experiences further support the findings of these studies. Involving our students in conferencing and reporting is well worth it.

Q. Our parents are so busy. They don't have time to come to school or to comment on things their kids are working on. How can we get them more involved?

R. Most parents want to help their children do well in school. And many parents do not have the time (or interest) to attend more meetings, be homework monitors, or read volumes of general messages coming from the school. We do find, however, that when their own children are the focus, parents are more likely to make the time. When students initiate conversations with their parents and talk about and show their own learning, adults stop and listen.

Conclusion

When we involve students in conferencing and reporting, they take a lead role by selecting and showing work samples, demonstrating skills, talking about their learning, and asking their audience for a response. "What counts" for us is that involving students in conferencing and reporting supports learning.

Conferencing and Reporting is the third book in the *Knowing What Counts* series, three books that describe ways of involving students in all aspects of assessment. The series also includes *Setting and Using Criteria* (book 1) and *Self-Assessment and Goal Setting* (book 2). The focus of each book is on classroom assessment practices that support learning for all students.

Appendix:
Reproducibles

The following pages may be reproduced for classroom use. To enlarge to 8½" x 11" (21.5 cm x 28 cm), please set photocopier at 143 percent, and align top edge of page with corresponding edge of copier glass.

Subject _____

Name _____

Table of Contents for _____

Select samples that show   **Your sample**

☐   a strength

☐   improvement

☐   successful collaboration

☐   originality

☐   other _____

Portfolio Afternoon **Audience Response**

Two compliments I have for _____ :

-

-

Something I would like to see next time:

-

Date _____   Signed _____

Portfolio Afternoon **Audience Response**

Two compliments I have for _____ :

-

-

Something I would like to see next time:

-

Date _____   Signed _____

Conferencing and Reporting, 2nd Edition, by K. Gregory, C. Cameron, and A. Davies
© 2001, 2011 • solution-tree.com

Goal Envelope for _____   **Response from** _____

Term _____ Subject(s) _____   Congratulations on:

My goal for this term is _____   -

_____

_____

My evidence shows I
- ☐ am working toward my goal
- ☐ have met my goal   -

1. _____   Next time:

2. _____

3. _____

Term _____ Subject(s) _____   **Response from** _____

Congratulations on:

My goal for this term is _____   -

_____

_____

My evidence shows I
- ☐ am working toward my goal
- ☐ have met my goal   -

1. _____   Next time:

2. _____

3. _____

Picture This

Place photo here

There is more to this picture than you can see. This is a photo

of_____

I/We want you to notice that:

\-

\-

\-

Date_____ Signed _____

Conferencing and Reporting, 2nd Edition, by K. Gregory, C. Cameron, and A. Davies
© 2001, 2011 • solution-tree.com

Response from _____

	It's Clear	It's Not Clear
1. After reading the criteria, I understand what was required in the assignment		
2. The criteria helped me see what you've done well		
3. I can see what you need to work on next		

Comments: _____

_____

_____

_____

Conferencing and Reporting, 2nd Edition, by K. Gregory, C. Cameron, and A. Davies
© 2001, 2011 • solution-tree.com

Headline:

Byline:

Dateline:

So far in _____ we have worked on the following:

-

-

-

I'm good at

I'm getting better at

I need to improve

Something I hope to do more of is

One word that describes my effort in class is

One thing I'd like to add is

Headline:

Byline:

Dateline:

So far in _____ we have worked on the following:

-

-

-

I'm good at

I'm getting better at

I need to improve

Something I hope to do more of is

One word that describes my effort in class is

One thing I'd like to add is

Conferencing and Reporting, 2nd Edition, by K. Gregory, C. Cameron, and A. Davies
© 2001, 2011 • solution-tree.com

Student-Parent-Teacher
Conferences

[School logo goes here]

Conferencing and Reporting, 2nd Edition, by K. Gregory, C. Cameron, and A. Davies
© 2001, 2011 • solution-tree.com

[SCHOOL NAME AND DATE)

Dear Parents/Guardians,

You are invited to attend a conference

on _____
DATE

At this time, the student, parent(s) and

teacher(s) will meet together to talk

about the learning that has taken place

during the term. The conference will

take 15 minutes. Your son/daughter

knows a great deal about his/her own

learning and has collected work

samples to show you.

By working together, we can support

your son or daughter's learning. I look

forward to seeing you at the

conference.

Yours truly,

_____
TEACHER SIGNATURE

Format

The number one purpose of the
conference is to support the learning
of your son or daughter by:

1. Talking about strengths and areas
   of progress

2. Looking at and discussing work
   samples

3. Talking about areas needing
   improvement

4. Setting one or two goals for next
   term

5. Discussing ways to help meet goals

* A written summary of the conversation
  will be sent home

Please return this portion

_____
Student's name

_____
Parent's name

Preferred days

☐ _____

☐ _____

Preferred time

☐ _____

☐ _____

Conferencing and Reporting, 2nd Edition, by K. Gregory, C. Cameron, and A. Davies
© 2001, 2011 • solution-tree.com

Student _____ Term _____

Subject _____ Date _____

Strengths/Accomplishments	**Work samples to show**
Areas needing improvement	**A goal for next term**

My closing statement: The most important thing I want you to know is . . .

Please note your conference is:

Date _____

Date _____ Time _____

Dear Parents/Guardians,

In preparation for our upcoming conference, please take a few minutes and jot down some ideas about your son or daughter. You might want to include accomplishments that take place outside of school as well as in school.

Yours truly,

_____
(TEACHER SIGNATURE)

Any areas of strength, growth, accomplishments:	One or two areas you'd like to see improvement in:	One specific goal:

P.S. Please bring these notes to the conference for your own use. Please do not send this form back to the school.

Conferencing and Reporting, 2nd Edition, by K. Gregory, C. Cameron, and A. Davies
© 2001, 2011 • solution-tree.com

Teacher Summary Sheet

Student_____ Term _____

Subject(s) _____ Date _____

Areas of strength	Areas needing improvement
	Additional notes:
Possible goal(s)	

Conferencing and Reporting, 2nd Edition, by K. Gregory, C. Cameron, and A. Davies
© 2001, 2011 • solution-tree.com

Parents/Guardians

We need your comments to improve our student-parent-teacher conferences. Thank you for taking the time to complete this form and return it to the school.

Two things you liked about the conference:

_____

_____

One suggestion:

_____

_____

One question:

_____

IEP Participant(s) Summary Sheet

Growth & development I've seen:

Practices that work well (at home, at school):

One or two areas to focus on next:

Bibliography

Angelo, T. A. & K. P. Cross. 1993. *Classroom Assessment Techniques: A Handbook for College Teachers* (2nd Edition). San Francisco: Jossey-Bass Publishers.

Black, P. & D. Wiliam. 1998. Assessment and classroom learning. *Assessment in Education* 5(1), 7–75.

Cameron, C., B. Tate, D. Macnaughton, & C. Politano. 1999. *Recognition Without Rewards*. Winnipeg, MB: Peguis Publishers.

Davies, A., C. Cameron, C. Politano, & K. Gregory. 1992. *Together Is Better: Collaborative Assessment, Evaluation, and Reporting*. Winnipeg, MB: Peguis Publishers.

Davies, A. 2011. *Making Classroom Assessment Work* (3rd Edition). Bloomington, IN: Solution Tree Press.

Gregory, K., C. Cameron, & A. Davies. 2011. *Self-Assessment and Goal Setting* (2nd Edition). Bloomington, IN: Solution Tree Press.

Gregory, K., C. Cameron, & A. Davies. 2011. *Setting and Using Criteria* (2nd Edition). Bloomington, IN: Solution Tree Press.

Henderson, A. & N. Berla. 1995. *A New Generation of Evidence: The Family Is Critical to Student Achievement*. Washington, DC: Center for Law and Education.

Jensen, E. 1998. *Teaching With the Brain in Mind*. Alexandria, VA: Association for Supervision and Curriculum Development.

Kohn, A. 1999. *The Schools Our Children Deserve*. New York: Houghton Mifflin.

Preece, A. 1995. Involving students in self-evaluation. In A. Costa and B. Kallick, *Assessment in the Learning Organization*. Alexandria, VA: Association for Supervision and Curriculum Development.

Stiggins, R. 2001. *Student-Involved Classroom Assessment,* 3rd Edition. Columbus, OH: Merrill Publishing.

Sutton, R. 1997. *The Learning School*. Salford, England: Sutton Publications.

Werner, E. & R. Smith. 1992. *Overcoming the Odds: High Risk Children From Birth to Adulthood*. Ithaca, NY: Cornell University Press.

Wiggins, G. 1993. *Assessing Student Performance: Exploring the Purpose and Limits of Testing*. San Francisco: Jossey-Bass Publishers.

Kathleen Gregory, BA, MEd, has more than 30 years' experience teaching at secondary, elementary, and middle schools. With a background in assessment practices and literacy strategies, she has also been a district curriculum coordinator and a support teacher for classroom teachers and school teams who are integrating students with special needs. A former teacher-in-residence at the University of Victoria, Kathleen is currently an instructor for literacy and assessment courses for pre-service teachers and is a consultant to many school districts in developing their own approaches to conferencing, reporting, and authentic assessment strategies.

Caren Cameron, MEd, has worked as a teacher, a District Principal of Educational Programs, and a sessional instructor at the University of Victoria. Currently she is an educational consultant working with school districts across Canada on a variety of topics including assessment and leadership. She is the co-author of a dozen practical books for colleagues, including a series for middle and primary years called *Voices of Experience*.

Anne Davies, PhD, is a researcher, writer, and consultant. She has been a teacher, school administrator, and system leader, and has taught at universities in Canada and the United States. She is a published author of more than 30 books and multi-media resources, as well as numerous chapters and articles. She is author or co-author of the best-selling books *Making Classroom Assessment Work*, the *Knowing What Counts* series, and the *Leaders Series*. A recipient of the Hilroy Fellowship for Innovative Teaching, Anne continues to support others to learn more about assessment in the service of learning and learners.